Time to Leave

Poems & Musings by Manaswini Srirangam

TIME TO LEAVE

Time to Leave

Poems & Musings by Manaswini Srirangam

Dedication

Our beloved, beautiful Manaswini,

Your writings always amazed us, but the true depth of your expression became even more evident after you ascended to higher planes. Each poem and musing you penned carries profound emotional and spiritual messages.

To celebrate our enduring and beautiful relationship and to honor your memory, we have compiled your works into this book. We trust that your words kindle introspection and touch the hearts and souls of many readers.

Manaswini, you were full of life, and the joy and love we shared will remain with us always. While your physical presence is deeply missed, we believe you are with us spiritually, constantly guiding us on our journey.

Ishtam♥, Manaswini Ma,
Grandmothers, Parents, Brother

Preface

We warmly invite you to enter the world of Manaswini Srirangam, our beloved beautiful daughter and sister — a humble soul and a gifted young writer whose words possess the deep ability to touch our hearts and stir our spirits. With great love and emotion, we share the collection of our child's writings, through this book, both in celebration of her brief yet joyful life and as a tribute to her memory.

Manaswini's writings reflect her deep love for her family and friends. In her work, life's subtle nuances, challenging stereotypes, empathetic and intuitive nature, and the profound philosophical insights she conveys, all shine through. Although being authored by a teenager, her works are marked by mature themes that resonate with both young adults and grown-ups. Collectively, they form an anthology that exudes greater insights, hope and mysticism.

As we fondly recall our cheerful daughter/sister and the warmth and joy she brought into our lives, we are deeply inspired by the lasting impressions she left on everyone who was part of her beautiful life's journey. In the "About the Author" section of this book, you will find excerpts from reflections shared by Manaswini's circle, offering glimpses into their shared journey with her and the cherished moments they spent together.

Now, as we explore the book's theme, butterflies come to the forefront. These delicate creatures symbolize transformation and joy, and they are often seen as messengers of angels. While Manaswini had great fascination for butterflies, since her journey to the celestial heights, we have consistently spotted yellow butterflies, among many, feeling an enduring connection to her through these beautiful beings. To us, the recurring presence of butterflies is a message that she remains close and is attempting to communicate. Thus, the book's overarching theme is butterflies!

To all our readers, we extend our heartfelt gratitude for choosing this book. Our hope is that you will find in Manaswini's words the same inspiration and resonance that we do, connecting with her enduring spirit through her writings.

Vasavi, Bala, and Srikar
(Mother, Father, Brother)

Introduction

This collection of writing by Manaswini Srirangam is a testament to how brightly she shone during her 17 years on this earth. Brimming with curiosity and an eagerness to understand the world around her, she was a keen observer of her surroundings, and she used her writing to process what she witnessed. Like any teenager stepping into adulthood, her life was going through an incredible transformation. As a chronicler of those changes, today she has left us with an incredible gift — a collection of her essays and poems that contain so much insight, wisdom, and guidance. Not only does this anthology help us process our grief, but also guides us on our own life's journey.

It is evident from reading her work that Manaswini possessed a wisdom far beyond her years. Take her poem, 'A Doll', where she talks about gender norms and bullying. It shows that she noticed the small details in life that others might have easily missed. Meanwhile, in her poem, 'The Curb', she guides us toward the understanding that fierce competition and human dominance will not serve humanity. She also did not shirk from expressing all the parts of life that were uncomfortable. In fact, she demonstrated how the act of writing would help transform these complicated emotions into an understanding that, in life, there are many dualities and truths that we straddle. She said it best in her poem 'Consumed' when she wrote, 'It is time that we finally accept that there is no perfect.' Perhaps, that acceptance is the closest we can all get to the notion of perfection.

Manaswini and I developed a relationship through handwritten letters exchanged with the help of her mother (my former colleague). We gushed about our shared love for LM Montgomery's Anne of Green Gables series. In the first book, the protagonist Anne Shirley, orphaned at birth, talks about her deep desire to connect with 'kindred spirits' and find a 'bosom buddy' — a friend whom she can hold close to her chest. Thankfully, she found that in her best friend, Diana. I can see Manaswini's own similar quest in her poem 'In Search', where she talks about looking for a kindred spirit, 'someone who has the same psychic wavelength as you'. In the tributes that have poured in from her friends and family, it is evident that she was that kindred spirit to so many.

Manaswini's absence leaves a gaping hole in the lives of her family and friends. With more time in this world, we can only wonder about how many more lives she would have touched with her radiant personality. We know that these writings will spread her magic even further. Even in her journey to celestial realms, she has taught us many valuable lessons, including the most important one: the impermanence of life. As she says in her own words, in the poem,

'Time to Leave': "There's a time limit to everything. Assignments have submission dates, medicines have expiry dates, and we have deadlines in life. That's just the way of the world."

Thank you, Manaswini, for everything.

Sindhuri Nandhakumar
Media professional and Pen Pal of Manaswini

As I laid on the damp, green grass,
I looked above at the twinkling stars across the night sky.
They looked like they were whispering to each other,
Trying to hold in the secrets of the universe.

I kept gazing at the stars,
Trying to figure it all out.
They say everything happens for a reason,
And that was all I wanted to know.

Manaswini Srirangam

Contents

Just not the
same

There are just those certain things
Which immediately give you comfort.
There are just those certain things
Which warm your heart at the slightest thought.

Your old teddy bear that you loved as a child,
The ring that you once considered your lucky charm,
Your old, tattered pair of sneakers
That you never could dispose of.

Yes, people grow up.
They outgrow teddies
Stop believing in charms
And find another pair of shoes.
But some things are just not the same.

There are just those certain things
Which pick you up when you feel low.
There are just those certain things
Which make you smile in the darkest of times.

Your old favourite playlist,
That one movie you loved to bits,
Your favourite person
That you were always around.

Yes, people move on and grow apart.
They find hundreds of new playlists
Thousands of new movies
And millions of new people.
But some things are just not the same.

There are just those certain things
Which ignite a fire within your heart and soul.
There are just those certain things
That you can never completely manage to let go.
As some things are simply, just not the same.

The Good Old Days

Sitting by the window, watching the heavy downpour
As nostalgia knocks on the door like an old friend
I begin reminiscing about the days
When I used to play 'which raindrop wins the race'
Carefree, oblivious to my surroundings.

After all, innocence is something that comes along with childhood
The day you mature, you leave everything behind –
innocence, freedom, and childhood
Never to walk down that road again.
All we have left with us are the memories.

Memories are things
Which remind you of the most beautiful and the happiest of
times.
Memories are things
Which give you all the joy in the world yet inflict the most pain.

Sitting by the window
Taking a walk down memory lane
I remember the day I learned to let go
The most beautiful, yet, the hardest day in my life.

Now, I've grown up
I have come to terms with the fact that I cannot go back
To the times when I was peaceful, blissfully ignorant
When we used to sing and play all day, without a care in the
world.

I still remember vividly
The day I walked out of the school gate one last time
I told myself that I have grown up
That I have to move on.

I could only look ahead, towards what the next day would bring to
the table
Hoping there would be, if not better, just as good times to be had
And I walked out with heavy eyes and a heavier heart
With memories of the 'good old days' etched into my soul, never
to be forgotten.

Hoping with all my might that there would be a day
When I look at whatever is to come as the 'good old days.'

Someday

We must have been about ten.
We were running around the place
Cycling, laughing, and talking about different things.
We thought it would last forever.
How naive.

Every time we met
Was our happy time.
If anybody had ever asked us what our happy place was
We would probably have said with each other.

We would come back from school everyday
And wait patiently for the clock to strike five
So that we could go play.
It was the happiest we had ever been.

Childhood is that part of your life
When you desperately want to grow up.
And once you've grown up
You want to go back to the 'good times.'

Just like everyone else
We imagined how our lives would be once we had grown up.
We decided that we would go to the same colleges
And even live close to each other.

Little did we know,
Life had something else in store for us.

We shifted to different places one day
As we had to move on in life.
We didn't know
That we wouldn't get a chance to ever look back.

And in that moment
We grew up.

We didn't like spending time away from each other
And now, we couldn't see each other.

We learnt what it is like to grow apart from your best friend.
They say distance makes your heart grow fonder – it is true.
We missed each other terribly and our hearts ached
But there was nothing we could do about it except plaster a smile on
our faces.

We did keep in touch through technology
But it is just not the same.
Eventually, we grew apart
Just like the others.

We learnt to live with it, over time
But we never forgot each other.
And just like that
We grew up, a little too quickly.

Even though we had our own separate lives
There wasn't a day when we didn't think of each other.
We woke up every single day with hope
That we would cross paths someday.

He had eyes like the stars
dreamy and brooding;
But it was that very pair of eyes
Which gave away everything he was hiding.

He would walk to school every day
And hope that he didn't cross paths with that one group of boys;
The ones who behaved like his friends
But he knew they only wanted his toys.

He once went to the toy store
And didn't take any time to think;
He picked out a pink Barbie doll
But Granny said, "Boys don't like dolls or pink."

She bought him a toy gun
And not the pretty, pink doll;
He didn't say a word but wondered
Why he was always expected to play with a ball.

He was different from the other boys
He didn't play a sport or a video game;
People around thought he was a weirdo
And slowly, to everyone, that's what he became.

He always worried that he didn't fit in
And was anxious about everything;
He would get bullied and pushed around
Only because he couldn't throw the basketball in the ring.

There were those few days
When he got beaten up really bad;
But Mum always told him
"Boys never cry or get sad."

By twelfth grade
He was the same height as any other girl;
He would be teased and made fun of
But to him, everything was just a whirl.

He had his own dreams and aspirations
That he wanted to chase;
But Dad enrolled him in an 'ideal' course
Because, after all, life is a race.

He went to college
Hoping it would be better there;
But soon enough he realized
People liked to fight with their hands, bare.

Being disrespectful to women
Was considered a fad;
He never took part in it
And for that, he was glad.

Many years passed
He now had a family;
He had decided long ago
That he would bring his children up differently.

He never let society get to him
And always gave it his all;
His daughter played with cars
And his son played with a doll.

A Doll

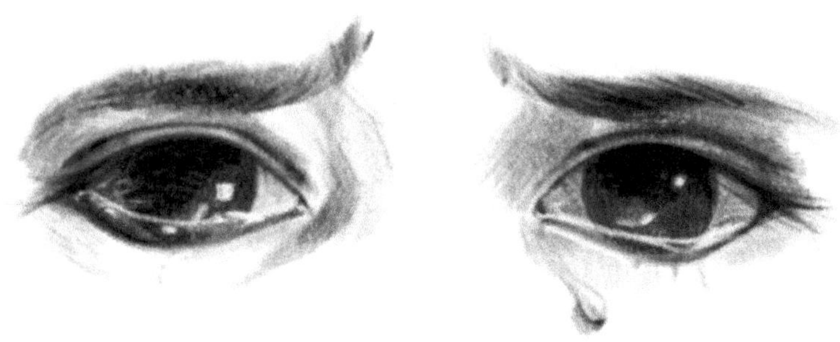

The Outcast 

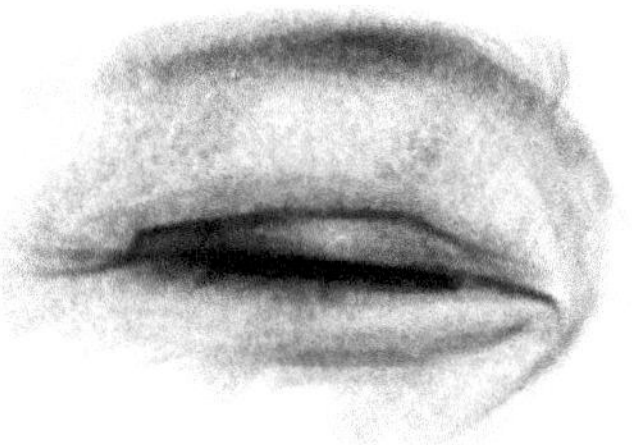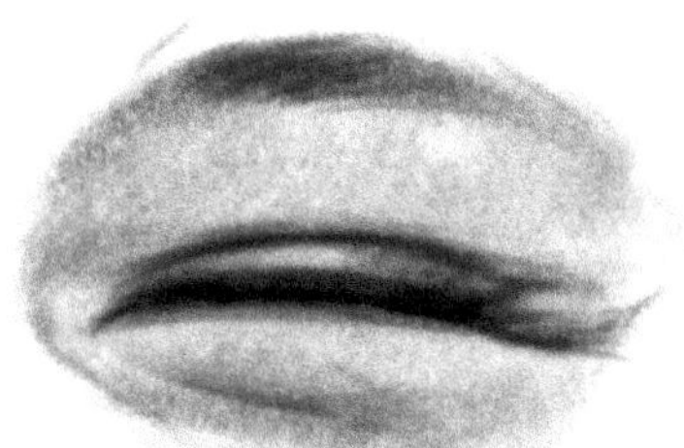

Fifth Grade.

I watched as the other girls played Tag, their screams and laughter echoing in my ears. One of the girls saw me looking and said, 'You're so weird, no wonder you don't have any friends.'

Mom came to pick me up after school.

'How was your day?' she asked.

Mom was always busy with work and worried about a lot of things. I didn't want to add to her already quite long list of worries. Good.' I said, blinking back tears.

Every single day was the same. I tried hard to fit in. But no matter what, I was always the outcast.

Seventh Grade.

We moved to another city for Mom's job, and naturally, I had to shift schools as well. I couldn't express the relief I felt when I heard we were moving. So, I remained silent. My silence was mistaken for sadness.

Mom sat me down and talked about how moving and growing distant from friends was a part of life. I nodded and managed a weak smile.

First Day of School.

I walked into the classroom nervously. The teacher asked me to introduce myself to the rest of the class, after which she told me to sit at the back of the class. As I walked to my desk, one of the kids tripped me, and as I fell, the entire class erupted in laughter. There were cries of Clumsy' and 'Klutz'.

I had been labelled on the very first day. And in school, labels are impossible to get rid of. Mom picked me up from school every day as usual. 'How was your day?' she'd ask.

'Good.' I'd say, plastering a smile on my face.

Ninth Grade.

We had to move to our hometown over the summer because Grandpa was ill. Mom was worried sick and was occupied in taking care of him most of the time.

First Day of School.

The new school was bigger than the previous one. The hallways and classrooms were cold and empty. And so were the people. The teacher introduced me to the class and told them to be nice. But one look at the kids, and you could tell − they were anything but that.

None of them would say a word. They would just stare at me, long and hard. Their eyes bore into mine expressionlessly. It was a regular reminder that I didn't belong here, among them.

I would sit in a corner of the classroom during lunch. Whenever I walked down the corridors, my eyes would be fixed on the floor. I would try to take up as less space as I could so as to not be noticed by people. I was as good as invisible.

I would walk home from school every day. I would always take the long route instead of the shortcut to avoid running into people from school. By the time I reached home, Mom would typically, be in the kitchen.

'How was your day?'

'Good.'

Eleventh Grade.

We moved back to the city we were in when I was in seventh grade. Chemotherapy didn't help Grandpa much − he didn't make it. Mom was almost always sad, but she did a good job trying to cover it up. The only reason I could see through it was because I did the same.

I was put in the same school as last time. At this point, moving to new schools and cities became second nature to me. I had given up all hope of fitting in and making friends. I was just getting through each day, one at a time.

First Day of School.

Old memories kept running through my head as I walked to my classroom. I prayed that nobody would recognize me. There were the usual introductions and then I walked to a desk at the back of the classroom, trying my hardest to make sure that there wouldn't be a reiteration of last time. Only this time, a girl walked up and sat next to me. She smiled brightly and introduced herself.

She helped me with stuff that I had missed as I joined a month late. I found it incredibly tough to digest the fact that someone was even talking to me, and that they were being nice. I thought she was pretending to be nice to me only as a prank. But I was wrong.

We sat together at lunch and talked about a lot of things. I didn't feel the need to behave like I didn't exist. We walked back home together after school – she lived in the street next to mine. At home, I found Mom on the sofa in the living room. She looked at me and smiled genuinely, after what seemed like ages.

'How was your day?' she asked.

'Good.' I smiled.

Nothing seemed to have changed really.
Except, this was the first time I meant it.

I wasn't an outcast, not anymore.

The Curb

Humans like to be in power
Irrespective of their age, gender, race
The natural instinct of human beings –
Dominance.

We enjoy the feeling of being superior to others, in any way.
People constantly keep comparing themselves to the ones
around them
To reassure themselves that they are good enough.
They enjoy the high they get from putting others down.

After all, society functions on the theory of the survival of the
fittest.
You must compete
And keep beating others while you are at it
To survive in this world.

This applies everywhere.
Humans happen to be at the top of quite a few food chains.
Even scientifically, we are at the top of the world.
The fate of other species is at our mercy.

Kids in school get bullied by bigger kids
We kill a bug
At the very sight of it.
There exists a hierarchy everywhere we go.

We thrive in throngs
In social groups.
We feel the need to belong somewhere
To survive yet another day in this cruel world.

And those of us who fail to follow norms
Those of us who are 'different'
Those of us who aren't considered 'normal'
Are ostracized by society.

After all,
Even The Law of The Jungle states
"The wolf that shall keep it may prosper,
But the wolf that shall break it must die."

It all boils down to power.
Power, influence, and status.
The ones who have it rule
And the ones who don't are kicked to the curb.

Better Days to Come

As the days go by
You cannot help but question the universe
"When will this end?"
"When will I feel whole again?"
The answer to your questions
Might not always be what you wanted to hear.

There may be times
When you are tired of it all
When all you want to do is just fall
Into deep, peaceful sleep.
The kind which heals
And you wake up feeling much better after.

You advise your friend
Who got her heart broken
"Time heals all wounds."
"You will be alright, there are better days to come."

How would you know
What it feels like
To be heartbroken
If you have never loved?

You call them fools
Or maybe they were 'being too naïve.'
And sometimes, you just don't know how to care for them
Because, after all,
How would you know
When you have never been in that situation yourself?

Sometimes, all people need
Is some empathy, love, and validation.
Validation that what they are going through is 'normal.'
Validation that it is not their fault
That they will be okay
That they, someday, might love again.

Usually, after something messy
They might not have the courage to love again
To go through all of it again.
At the end of the day
Feelings are exhausting.

They drain you of all energy
And sometimes, hope.
But ironically, the only thing that keeps you going
Is hope.

Hope that there will be better days.
Hope that you will learn to love again.

Why is it that
We want the things we can't have?
Why is it that
We blatantly refuse to give up on the very things that crush us?

It's funny how
The more we don't get something
The more that becomes the centre of our attention
And is subject to our complete effort.

It's funny how
We take months and months trying to get over someone
Who didn't think of you for even a fraction of the time
You spent pining for them.

It's funny how
The people we used to admire and idolize
Fall so hard from their pedestals
Which were so high up in our minds.

It's funny how
Someone so very easily
Walks all over your heart
In high-heeled boots.

But then again
If you were in their place
You would do the same.
Wouldn't you?

It is funny.
Isn't it?

Funny

Lost
in the Crowd

As I sit among all these people
I feel a wave of sadness hit.
I try to suppress it
And try to hide my face.

But soon enough
I realise that no one cares.

So, I give in
And succumb to weakness.
A tear rolls down my cheek
A sigh escapes my lips.

When I'm satisfied
I wipe that lone tear
And plaster a fake smile on my face
Again.

I am just another person
Lost in the crowd.

Little
do you know

Every time the hurricane in her heart threatens to surface
She rocks her body between her arms
With such force that fatigue consumes her
And she falls into shallow sleep
Safe from herself
For a meagre few hours.

But little do you know
This is only the calm before the storm.

35

There are times when I have nothing in particular to think about
My brain decides to go on a thinking spree, trying to contemplate life.
It was during one such instance that this sudden thought struck me
Everything, and everyone, is replaceable.

When you order something online, and you aren't satisfied with it
You replace it with something else that you think is better.
Remember the first friends you made in kindergarten?
Well, you grew up.

It pretty much works the same way with people too.
You meet people, hang out with them, and when you get bored of them
You begin ignoring them and completely cut off from them.
You find someone that, you think, is better
and replace the former with the latter.

And the cycle repeats itself.
This made me realize how easy it is to replace someone or something.
Things and people hold no value anymore.
Everything, and everyone, is replaceable.

You meet someone, you fall in love
You find someone else, you move on.
You replaced a person.
Everything, and everyone, is replaceable.

Somebody dear to you dies
You grieve their death for a while.
You find someone that you now hold dearer to you.
Everything, and everyone, is replaceable.

Every single one of us is guilty of replacing something, or someone
At some point in our lives, sometimes multiple.
There is no value left of anything, or anyone, anymore
As everything, and everyone, is replaceable.

Irreplaceable *or* Replaceable?

Is it just me or does everybody feel
An inner void that they need to conceal
Don't let it show, that's the deal
We must all put up a front that we are made of steel.

A void is a large space that is vacant
Where the self turns into its own assailant
It needs to be dealt with courage, grit, and patience
And has to be under constant surveillance.

The void is an inner voice that echoes my insecurities
And makes me think of all the catastrophic possibilities
It puts me in a situation of complete obscurity
Not letting it get to me is an absolute rarity.

Only few of us are in blissful ignorance
Of the void's very existence
All of us resort to putting up a facade
To cover up the fact that everyone is flawed.

We find it hard to admit
And it takes all our spirit
To bring to light our flaws
Which needn't be done without a cause.

It is time that we finally accept
That there is no perfect
Therefore, in retrospect
It is an issue we cannot neglect.

As humanity would be doomed
If by the void, we are to be consumed.

Consumed

Why is it that
Hope is one of the most important reasons for your existence
Yet it is hope that
Shatters your very being every second of your life.

It is said that a person can survive
Four weeks without food
Four days without water
But he cannot survive even four seconds without hope.

People do not die due to depression
Or anxiety
Or even suicide
They die due to the lack of hope.

If you believe that you do not want to live
try throwing yourself into a river
You will find yourself fighting
Your lungs will scream for air
And every part of your body will beg to live.

This is because human beings are programmed.
Hope is etched into our souls, minds, and hearts
And it is hard to convince ourselves otherwise.

We are programmed in such a way that
No matter how many times we face failure, rejection or are
walked over
Even after being let down countless times
We have hope left for a miracle.

You know that people truly are on the brink of hopelessness
When you notice their smiling lips, but soulless eyes.

Hope gives you all the reasons to live
But leaves you hurting so bad
That you begin to question whether you want to lead
such a painful life.

Hope is a double-edged sword.

Double-edged *Sword*

Without Remorse

There once was a girl who had it all
She was smart, brave, and as pretty as a doll
Her eyes shone as brightly as the stars scattered
across the night sky
She always got through the day with her head held high.

But all of a sudden, her eyes lost their spark
She found herself beginning to seek shelter in the dark
She started longing for appreciation
And in all of her endeavours, needed validation.

She always tried to please people
And was walked over by multiple
Until one day, she realized
It was only if she loved herself completely
Would she be able to love another unconditionally.

You cannot find happiness and solace in an external source
One must learn to find it within to live without remorse.

The *Mirror*

I looked into the mirror
Only to see her staring back
Her eyes bore into mine
Her face, expressionless.

I didn't know her, not anymore.
All I saw was a girl
Scarred by her past
Scared to witness her future.

Every chance she got
She put herself under scrutiny.
The body and soul were at war
Resulting in the loss of tranquillity.

She would hide the scars
Visible and otherwise, from the world
Afraid that she was inadequate
That she had no place in social hierarchy.

She was tired of everything
Her fears
Her life
And her own self.

She wanted to end it all
And she did.
It worked just how slow poison does
Taking its own, sweet time.

After all,
That's how healing works.
It takes all the time in the world
But renders you changed.
The only difference is, the former leaves you lifeless
While the latter leaves you full of life.

A year later, I look into the mirror again
And I see her
Smiling back at me
Her face radiant.

She ended her old self, her insecurities and life
To embrace a new one.
Like a phoenix,
She rose from her own ashes.

45

They say there is somebody out there
To whom your heart you can bare
But I didn't think there was anybody with whom I could share
Everything I had to say without them getting a scare.

And there you came along
I wanted to believe that we would prove to be strong
But clearly, I turned out to be wrong
I had lost you in the throng.

It was like you had disappeared into thin air
As if you had never been there
I trusted you with my soul, I swear
But I still wanted to know how you would fare.

When I needed you the most, you weren't around
I tried to express it, but couldn't make a sound
I wanted to gesture, but I was bound
By rigid, invisible ropes creeping up from the ground.

Now, all I can do is just wait around
And be patient, until one day, the 'somebody' comes round.

Bound

As I laid on the damp, green grass
I looked above at the twinkling stars across the night sky
They looked like they were whispering to each other
Trying to hold in the secrets of the universe.

Keeping a secret is hard
But probably not to those who are used to bottling it up
The ones who hold back weren't always the same
They learnt over time that some things are better left unsaid.

I kept gazing at the stars
Trying to figure it all out.
They say everything happens for a reason
And that was all I wanted to know.

With the music blasting in my ears
I kept thinking over and over.
From the corner of my eyes, I saw the silhouette of an old
man approaching
And I looked over distractedly.

His eyes seemed to stare into my soul
And in that moment, I felt vulnerable.
He just smiled, the corners of his eyes crinkling as he did so
And breathed – 'Just hold on.'
I kept looking at him, confused
Until he pointed to the sky.

For the first time in my life
I saw a shooting star.
Not caring about being perceived as naïve
I made a wish upon it.

I turned back to look at the man
Only to find not a single soul.

My eyes fixated themselves on the night sky once more
With a million thoughts running through my head.
I didn't know if my wish would come true
But I realised – to find out, I had to 'just hold on.'

Now, looking back, I don't know
If I truly saw either the shooting star, or the man
But I would like to believe so.

Just Hold *On*

As I talk to you
My eyes keep wandering distractedly
Looking for a kindred spirit, perhaps.

A kindred spirit is one
Who is on the same psychic wavelength as you.
Someone who just gets you
Without you ever having to try hard.

When you are with them
It all just flows.
You are at peace
And everything in the world feels alright.

Even if it's not the case
You feel carefree.
All your worries disappear temporarily
For the extent of time that you spend with them.

But the one thing with having a kindred spirit in your life is
They become such an important part of your life
That you cannot imagine
What it would be like without them.

Sometimes,
You don't even realise that you found them.
And you keep searching
While they are right under your nose.

I realize in this moment
That I have spent my whole life looking for one.
I haven't found one yet.
Or have I?

In Search

51

I remember when I was in my first year of kindergarten, I had quite a hard time. Most of it was just my three-year-old self bawling her eyes out at being separated from her mom.

I got attached to my class teacher. It was like I felt a void while at school and I looked for something to fill it. For me, it took the form of my teacher. I used to follow her around and would refuse to leave her alone for a single moment. I imagine that was due to the fear of abandonment. Of course, I got over it and things were good from the following year.

I am seventeen years old now. I am at university, and I would practically be moving out soon. If my mom was to be asked, she would say that I am not very attached to my family and wouldn't miss them one bit. I might give off that impression sometimes, but the truth is quite far from it really. I would also have to leave my friends, the people who keep me sane, behind.

I thought I would enjoy moving out and not look back, but the closer it gets, the more nervous I feel. Maybe it is because I must start all over again. Afresh. I know when that day finally arrives, I will feel three years old again.

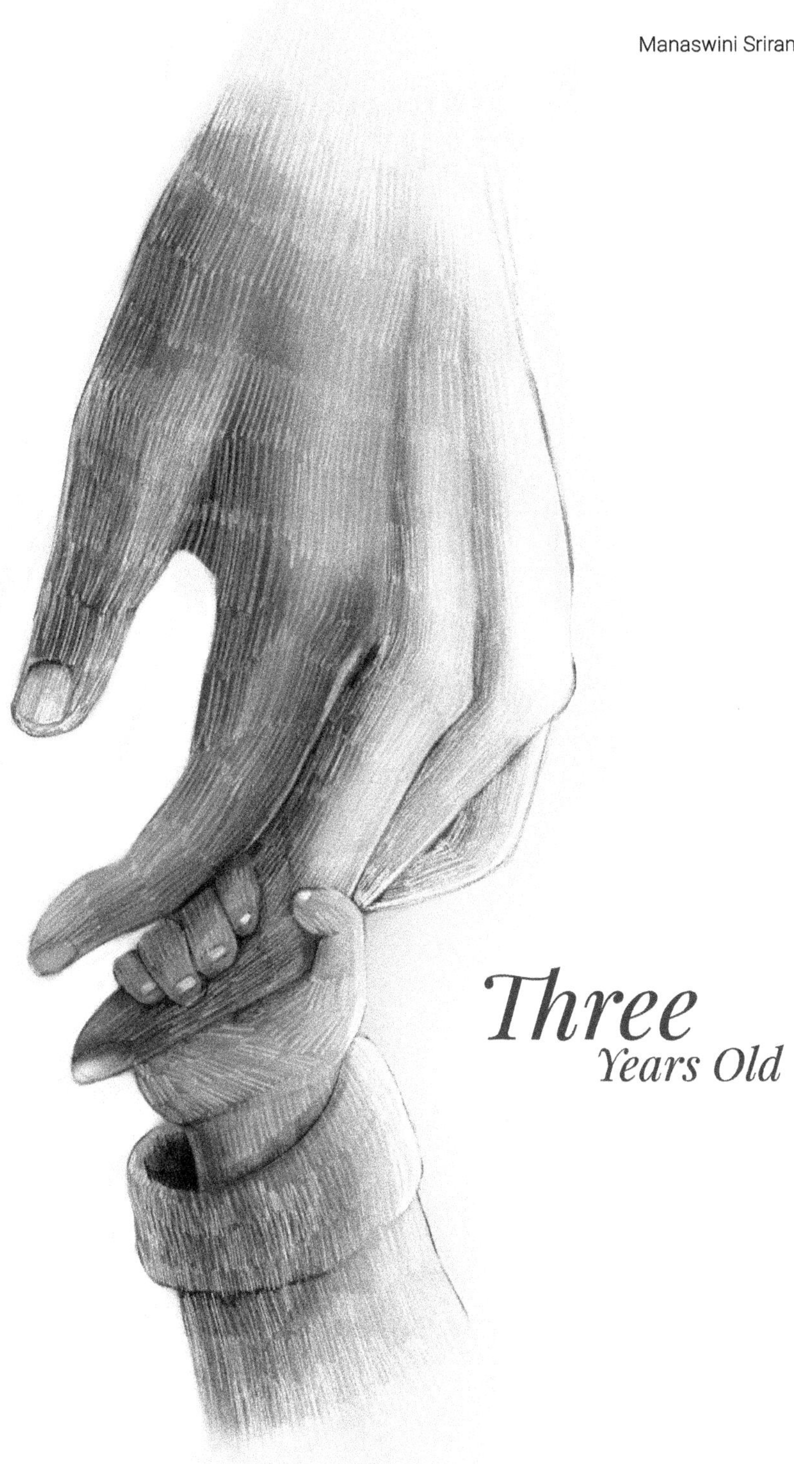

Three
Years Old

Let Go

We cross paths with people from different walks of life. Every person we meet either gives us beautiful memories to cherish or teaches us a lesson. But it is the people that one doesn't expect, who end up turning their backs on them.

It does not do one any good to get emotionally attached or be emotionally dependent on people, because life is unpredictable. The only constant is change. People change all the time. It is hard to trust anyone or everyone. In the end, the people that you trusted with your heart and soul are the ones who hurt you.

It is not only the significant things which matter. The smallest and most insignificant details need to be paid attention to as well. It is a fact that actions, do indeed, speak louder than words. It does not do to blindly trust the words that people say. Their actions reflect most of their thoughts/feelings. It is quite easy to fabricate thoughts in the form of words, but it is the actions of a person which truly reflect their deepest beliefs.

In the process that we call life, there may be times when we get exhausted. The hurt and pain may become too much to handle. We may feel broken beyond repair. Nothing may seem to make it better. But must remember our goals, dreams, and ambitions in life. We worked hard and reached where we are in life, not to turn back. We must keep going. Let the fire in you burn brighter. Keep reminding yourself why you are doing what you are doing.

No grudges or hard feelings must be held against the people who hurt you either. Everything in life is an experience. The only reason you are who you are today is because of all that you have gone through.

Everything that you experience in life just makes you a better person. You are a better person today than you were yesterday. You must keep refining yourself, to be the best version of yourself that you can be.

'Forgive and Forget' must be the motto in life. You must learn to forgive others for the things they have done and forget about it.

It is important to know who in your life are really the ones who can be trusted. Keep these people close and never let go. But at the same time, never set your happiness on one person, or a group of people.

Never let others be in control of your happiness or emotions.
Never get emotionally attached. Emotionally detach and let go.

As a kid, the concept of goodbyes
Was always devastating.
We would go to my grandparents' house every year with all of our
cousins
And we would spend lots of time together.
Yet, when the time came to leave,
We would bawl.

Why do we have to leave,
I always wondered.
Why couldn't we just stay here, together,
And be happy all the time?

Every time I asked my mother that
She would just say
"All of us have our own lives to get back to."
I would refuse to accept that.

My younger self did not understand then that,
That's not how life works.
We do not stay happy all the time
At the same time, we do not remain eternally sad either.
It is important to go through each and every emotion
That we feel in every moment.

After going back home
I would feel low for a while.
I would wish that we didn't have to come back.
But eventually, everything would go back to normal.

Once I got a little older
I understood it all.

There's a time limit to everything.
Assignments have submission dates,
Medicines have expiry dates,
And we have deadlines in life.
That's just the way of the world.

After this realization dawned upon me
I learnt to savour every moment, happy or sad.
We would always depart with wide grins
When it was time to leave.

Time
to Leave

57

"Little did we know
Life had something else in store for us."

'Someday' by Manaswini Srirangam

About the Author

Manaswini Srirangam
April 8, 2004 — February 24, 2022

Manaswini Srirangam, born in Mumbai in April 2004, lived all 17 years of her life in Chennai, India.

An alumnus of DAV and NPS International Schools, Chennai, Manaswini nurtured a deep passion for an array of disciplines within the literary and liberal arts world, spanning Psychology, Sociology, Philosophy, Literature, and Media and Communication. This passion led her to pursue her undergraduate degree in B.A. Honours in Aesthetics and Peace Studies at the prestigious Manipal University, a program that seamlessly blends Liberal Arts and Social Sciences.

From her childhood, she was fascinated with books. She began reading at the age of three and quickly became an avid reader by the time she entered Primary School. Her effortless reading of storybooks amazed both her kindergarten teacher and classmates.

Manaswini cherished a diverse range of genres, including fiction, nonfiction, thrillers, psychological, mythological, and philosophical works. Some of her favourite books at different stages of her life included classics like 'Anne of Green Gables' by LM Montgomery, the magical world of 'Harry Potter' by JK Rowling, the coming-of-age gem 'The Perks of Being a Wallflower' by Stephen Chbosky, and the gripping 'The Silent Patient' by Alex Michaelides.

She developed the habit of writing from her early days and won accolades in intra and inter-school competitions. If she wasn't spending time with her family or friends, you would find her either writing or reading. Driven by her love for music, she tried her hand at mastering the Veena.

She became an ardent fan of Japanese Anime in her later years. She enjoyed a good sitcom and would quote one-liners from her favourite shows like Friends, Brooklyn Nine-Nine and Good Witch. If anyone wanted to strike up a conversation about Harry Potter, Anime, Friends or K-Dramas, she was their go-to person.

Her university journey in 2021 had started with a lot of excitement and anticipation. During the brief period that she was at the Uni, she won various accolades and had the opportunity to host various webinars in the fields of Ecosophy and Arts. She aspired to a career in international non-profit organizations like the UN after completing her double masters in Peace Studies and International Relations.

Exploring facets of her personality, she identified herself as an ambivert. Family and friends meant the world to her. She loved meeting new people and making new friends yet felt most comfortable with the people closest to her. She was a fun-loving and adventurous person, always ready to embrace new challenges.

With a gentle and composed personality, Manaswini lived by the principles of Empathy, Hope, and Happiness—qualities that endeared her to everyone she met. Yet, it seemed the Gods loved her even more.

Family

Mesmerising as a person, Adorable and awesome, Nice and full of love, Attitude is like a dove, Sweet with everyone, Wonderful to the scale of ten, Intelligent and beautiful, Nature so sweet and joyful, Intention always truthful. Manaswini, you are our little pole star, Twinkling brightly in the sky, Guiding us all in the dark.
Uma Atha, Narayana Mavayya, Nikhil, Nithya

From a happy and carefree child, Manaswini grew into a positive, fun-loving, eloquent girl with a maturity beyond her age. She earned the affection of many friends and well-wishers with her genial nature. Her zest for life, and bright smile are etched in our hearts and will be cherished forever!
Purnima Atha, Hari Mavayya, Shruti, Shreya

Calm, sincere, and a kind-hearted girl; cracked your way to use your talents for the good. You were the key to unlocking healing for your family and friends. Your poems have deeper meaning reflecting your philosophical bent of mind. We can see it flowing truly from the bottom of your heart, depicting the reality of today's life and times.
Madhavi Dodda, Mahesh Pedanaanna, Sidharth, Srujana

Always knew you as a masterpiece,
Never knew you can write so well with ease.
Wish the world saw of you a lot more,
Through this you will live with us ever more.
You lived big, and we all take a bow.
Bobby Mama, Swati Atha, Shriaansh, Akshara

Teachers

The sweet smile, sparking eyes, who liked to play small pranks!
The never give up attitude, who had great gratitude for the small joys in life. The sensible child who accepted her limitations and worked towards overcoming them. The gentle soul who cared enough to want to make a positive difference, even if a small one, in people's lives.
Priya Aunty

The day you walked into Sweety Pies, dressed in a cute little frock, your smile brightened our lives. The love, hugs, and kisses you shared, made me feel you were my own lovely little daughter.
Pavithra Ma'am

It was a pleasure to be a part of Manaswini's high school years. She was a charming child with a cute smile and a cheerful one in her group.
A vibrant part of an ever-enthusiastic IXC, XC (2017 ÷ 2019).
Shubhaa Madhavan Ma'am

When it came to Manaswini's turn to introduce herself to the class, the other six-year-old students automatically put their hands over their mouth and said with awe, "Oh! She has Ma'am's name!" I caught Manaswini smiling her quiet smile, but she gave away no other expression. She was a teacher's dream because the skills were already in place, and one only had to fine tune them ever so little. Manaswini never displayed pride as I did so, and because of that, the other students were willing to accept her as a role model.
Manaswini Ma'am

Manaswini made her presence felt with her quirky remarks and dry sense of humour, and quickly became an irreplaceable member of the class. We had interesting conversations on topics ranging from Economics, History, Politics, Friendship, and life in general. I always appreciated Manaswini's candor and ability to articulate. She was well-read and this was evident in her ability to chip into any conversation that she was part of. Manaswini, this book is testament to your creativity and might of the pen.
Ranjani R Ayyar Ma'am

Manaswini, a student with rare qualities. She is permanently etched in my memory.
Anonymous

Friends

"The person who held my hand when I was dropped by the rest, the one who reminds me of my childhood at its best. From animated books to crosswords, we have come a long way — from baby steps to soaring towards our dreams, you never made hardships stay." Manu always had my back in school. She stood for me even when no one else was around, raising trust and giving hope. She made me realize that it's not about how many, but who stands by you. Manu is always kind and truly one of a kind.
Vaishnavi Jagannathan

Walking along the corridors
sharing laughs over lunch
fighting for silly reasons
gifting each other our old pens.
We went from being strangers
to becoming TBFF (True Best Friends Forever).

She taught me a lot
to listen to one's inner voice
to let go of ego
she was like a butterfly
spreading happiness wherever she goes.
Varsheni Padmanabhan

In our trio, while Dharna would be the overly emotional and Vidhi the equally emotionless, Manas would be the rational voice. In times of crisis (mainly boy talks and school dramas, for our young teen selves), she would offer her motherly perspective and mature advice. Manas was a creative soul. Her calm and gentle aura was her charm. She was sensitive in her understanding of the world and extremely reliable. She will always be an inseparable part of this "chaos" that our 9th grade selves chose to call "The Three Musketeers."
Dharna Bafna and Vidhi Srivastava

You were one of the kindest, wholesome and one of the most amazing people I have ever met in my life. You were there for me when I was at my lowest, when I needed to get advice, and when I needed a shoulder to cry on. You gave yourself to everyone, you let others into your warmth even when you were not in high spirits. You were everyone else's spirit, and the beacon of light.
Prusha Bhat

Manaswini was the most caring, fun-loving, and understanding person I know. She deeply cared about all her friends and was very mature for her age. She was always fun to be around, and it was easy to talk to her about anything. She had the prettiest smile that always lit up the room, she will always be in our hearts forever! I love you Manu, always and forever.
Tharuniyaa Lakshmi

She always looks at the brighter side of things fearlessly even when things are falling apart. She was the beacon of light amid our darkest nights. Trusting, loving and being warm, hope for many, special person, and a beautiful friend!
Sidharth Mohan

Mannu was a real good friend of mine, a very mature and loving girl. I wasn't lucky enough to spend a lot of time with her, but we made the best of it. She was a very good listener and a great writer. It's going to be hard to live in a world without you, Mannu!
Sanjay Saravanan

A soulful person, elegant, eloquent, and extremely articulate in expressing her thoughts in simple words. In the darkest of nights, Manaswini brings colour to life! From dolls to the flaws in humanity, everything has been expressed in such a way that every word can be related to all our experiences. This book is nothing but a beautiful collection! I will miss the conversations we had about Harry Potter and the fact that we both loved the same line, "After all this time?" "Always."
Sundar Karthikeyan

Writing that truly reflects the reality and complexity of our teenage lives, often overlooked by adults who don't truly understand our world. Breaking norm and normalcy, Mannu's poetry explores the best and worst of teen life. Truly missed but never forgotten!
Rakshan Purushothaman

Manaswini was very compassionate, she would be there for all of us, to hear us out and comfort. She was very patient. We had so much of fun in our 11th grade, did a lot of naughty stuff together. She was an absolute joy, I'm glad that we were friends.
Taruni Dintakurti

Manaswini is someone who puts you at ease quickly; she is the one person who can genuinely be happy for you, wholeheartedly support you, and truly wish well for you. It's quite rare to see such qualities in this world which makes me extremely proud and lucky to have met Manaswini. Her life, her memories, her poems, and her personality will never ever be forgotten. She was a gem of a person.
Aashna Srikrishnan

Wini, you are and will always be one of the kindest, funniest, and most loving souls I have ever met. I will fondly remember the times we spent together, taking turns to read our old poems to each other. You always had a way with words; it felt like they came out of you with pure emotion, which is something I know people struggle with — to be so vulnerable with your words and yet find strength and comfort in them.
Velika E. Shangpliang

Wini was a kind human being, intelligent, silent, mature, sensitive, helpful, into K-Pop and desired to pursue International Relations.
We were together in a team to write content. She was always ready with her work and would do even my part at times. I can picture her eating Lays, phone in one hand and sitting with her legs folded to the right side on Veli's side of the bed.
Alice Chauhan

I have never met a girl so pure and kind in my life. One beautiful memory I have of Wini is when she got so excited seeing me perform Kathak; she was very enthusiastic about learning this dance form in her life.
Aakarshika Singh

2021 was the beginning of our college life at Manipal, a place that excited all of us to the core. Initially, we had our classes online.
One random day Wini texted me saying 'hi' and how cool she found me in class, specifically mentioning that she adored me for my ambition of being a pilot. She was never an insecure person, nor did she ever refrain from complimenting people for their tiniest achievements. We had our first ever solo flights together, that's how I'll always keep you in my heart, like a beautiful memory and my partner in a little adventure.
Suhani Rajpoot

Wini was one of the first friends I made in college. I actually got pretty intimidated, because she seemed so articulate. I was amazed by how she knew exactly how to put her ideas across, but as I got to know her more personally she revealed herself as the purest and most welcoming person.
Chinmayee Balkar

K Shravan S Basri

Acknowledgements

Publishing the works of our beloved daughter, Manaswini Srirangam, was a heartfelt decision born from deep reflection. We embarked on this journey with the hope that her simple yet profound thoughts on life and beyond will resonate and inspire others as they have inspired us. Thus, Time to Leave was born. The unwavering support and encouragement from family, friends, and even kind-hearted strangers made this endeavor a reality.

This journey, though challenging, has been enriched with beautiful lessons and the support of many. We express our deepest and most sincere gratitude to everyone who walked with us on this path and would like to take this opportunity to specifically acknowledge a few.

We feel blessed to be part of a family whose love, support, and understanding have been the guiding light throughout this journey. In moments of quiet reflection and during the most challenging times, they stood by us, offering strength, encouragement, and an unshakeable faith that carried us forward.

Vijaya Karra, our aunt and an accomplished author, has been a constant source of support throughout this journey. Her steadfast encouragement and insightful guidance helped us stay focused and move forward. It's hard to imagine this book coming to life without her support.

We extend our immense gratitude to Sindhuri Nandakumar, Manaswini's pen pal, for her invaluable contribution to this book and for considerately writing the eloquent introduction.

We are deeply grateful to the teachers, friends, and family who shared their beautiful memories of Manaswini, enabling us to capture them permanently in this collection.

We thank Centrick, whose contribution and support brought the author's work to life through their Ilustrations and book composition.

Our sincere thanks to the team at Notion Press for their support in bringing this book into the world. It means so much to us, and we deeply appreciate their expertise in guiding its journey to publication. Finally, we express our gratitude to you, the reader, for embracing this book with your love.

A special mention goes to our son, Srikar Srirangam, whose beautiful butterfly artwork adorns the inner pages of this book, symbolizing our connection with Manaswini. We love you, Srikar. Above all, we deeply cherish the love and divine blessings of our child, which have made it possible to share her works with the world. We love you, Manaswini.

In memory of Manaswini, we have established the Manaswini Smruthi Foundation **msf.yr18@gmail.com**, a family-owned and managed organization dedicated to transforming lives through education and meaningful relief initiatives. This book is dedicated to supporting the Foundation's mission, with proceeds from every sale contributing to our efforts.

With much gratitude!

We,
her proud parents.

"Zindagi badi honi chahiye, lambi nahi"

You may not have lived long but have certainly lived BIG!
You came, you saw, you loved, you inspired,
and we pray that through this book,
you reach out to many more and conquer it all.

Gone too soon but you will remain forever in our hearts.

Swati Atha

Ishtam